# OWL WISDOM

### Zoe Bell

summersdale

Summersdale Publishers Ltd
46 West Street
Chichester
West Sussex
PO19 1RP
UK

www.summersdale.com

Printed and bound in the Czech Republic

ISBN: 978-1-84953-874-9

Substantial discounts on bulk quantities of Summersdale books are available to corporations, professional associations and other organisations. For details contact Nicky Douglas by telephone: +44 (0) 1243 756902, fax: +44 (0) 1243 786300 or email: nicky@summersdale.com.

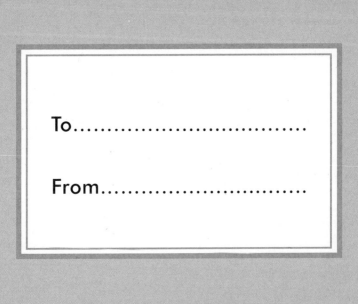

To.....................................

From.................................

Whatever you can do or dream you can, begin it. Boldness has genius, power and magic in it.

**JOHANN WOLFGANG VON GOETHE**

Let your hook
always be cast; in
the pool where you
least expect
it, there will be fish.

OVID

Love yourself first
and everything else
falls into line.

**LUCILLE BALL**

I can't change the
direction of the wind,
but I can adjust my sails
to always reach my
destination.

**JAMES DEAN**

Opportunities are like
sunrises. If you wait too
long, you miss them.

**WILLIAM ARTHUR WARD**

*If you're going
to be thinking
anything, you might
as well think big.*

**DONALD TRUMP**

If we had no winter,
the spring would not
be so pleasant.

ANNE BRADSTREET

He has achieved
success who has lived
well, laughed often,
and loved much.

**BESSIE ANDERSON STANLEY**

All life is an experiment.
The more experiments you
make the better.

**RALPH WALDO EMERSON**

You only get one
chance at life and you
have to grab it boldly.

**BEAR GRYLLS**

*Be faithful to that which exists nowhere but in yourself.*

ANDRÉ GIDE

Don't save things for a
special occasion. Every
day of your life is a
special occasion.

**THOMAS S. MONSON**

Things do not
happen. Things are
made to happen.

**JOHN F. KENNEDY**

Life is a great big canvas; throw all the paint you can at it.

DANNY KAYE

There is nothing
impossible to him
who will try.

**ALEXANDER THE GREAT**

Go as far as you can
see; when you get
there, you'll be able
to see further.

**THOMAS CARLYLE**

When life looks like it's
falling apart, it may just
be falling in place.

**BEVERLY SOLOMON**

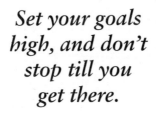

*Set your goals high, and don't stop till you get there.*

BO JACKSON

It's all right to have butterflies in your stomach. Just get them to fly in formation.

ROB GILBERT

Follow your own star!

**DANTE ALIGHIERI**

Wherever you go, no matter
what the weather, always
bring your own sunshine.

**ANTHONY J. D'ANGELO**

Opportunity does not knock,
it presents itself when you
beat down the door.

**KYLE CHANDLER**

*Enthusiasm*
*moves the world.*

ARTHUR BALFOUR

You can, you should,
and if you're brave
enough to start, you will.

**STEPHEN KING**

When you're true to
who you are, amazing
things happen.

**DEBORAH NORVILLE**

The man who
removes a
mountain
begins by
carrying away
small stones.

CHINESE PROVERB

I have found that if
you love life, life will
love you back.

**ARTHUR RUBINSTEIN**

For myself I am an optimist – it
does not seem to be much
use being anything else.

**WINSTON CHURCHILL**

Mix a little foolishness
with your serious plans.
It is lovely to be silly at
the right moment.

**HORACE**

*Where there is great love there are always miracles.*

**WILLA CATHER**

**One way to get the most out of life is to look upon it as an adventure.**

WILLIAM FEATHER

If you think you are
too small to make a
difference, try sleeping
with a mosquito.

**DALAI LAMA**

If you don't like how
things are, change it!
You're not a tree.

**JIM ROHN**

Do not wait: the
time will never be
'just right'.

**NAPOLEON HILL**

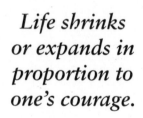

*Life shrinks
or expands in
proportion to
one's courage.*

**ANAÏS NIN**

It is in your moments
of decision that your
destiny is shaped.

**TONY ROBBINS**

To fight fear, act.
To increase fear –
wait, put off, postpone.

**DAVID JOSEPH SCHWARTZ**

# Our best successes often come after our greatest disappointments.

HENRY WARD BEECHER

Always laugh when
you can. It is cheap
medicine.

**LORD BYRON**

Aerodynamically the bumble bee shouldn't be able to fly, but the bumblebee doesn't know it so it goes on flying anyway.

**MARY KAY ASH**

Tell me, what is it you plan
to do with your one wild
and precious life?

**MARY OLIVER**

*Life is a helluva lot more fun if you say yes rather than no.*

RICHARD BRANSON

The **best way** to predict your future is to create it.

ABRAHAM LINCOLN

In dreams and in
love there are no
impossibilities.

**JÁNOS ARANY**

No great thing is
created suddenly.

**EPICTETUS**

Don't judge each
day by the harvest
you reap but by the
seeds that you plant.

**ROBERT LOUIS STEVENSON**

*Everything in
our life should be
based on love.*

**RAY BRADBURY**

Setting goals is the
first step in turning the
invisible into the visible.

**TONY ROBBINS**

A happy life consists
not in the absence,
but in the mastery of
hardships.

**HELEN KELLER**

**Opportunity dances with those already on the dance floor.**

H. JACKSON BROWN JR

The thing to do is
enjoy the ride while
you're on it.

**JOHNNY DEPP**

Mistakes are the
portals of discovery.

**JAMES JOYCE**

What we need is more
people who specialise
in the impossible.

**THEODORE ROETHKE**

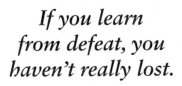

*If you learn
from defeat, you
haven't really lost.*

ZIG ZIGLAR

# Angels can fly because they take themselves lightly.

G. K. CHESTERTON

It takes courage to
grow up and become
who you really are.

E. E. CUMMINGS

Shoot for the moon.
Even if you miss, you'll
land among the stars.

**LES BROWN**

Throw caution to the
wind and just do it.

**CARRIE UNDERWOOD**

*Opportunities
multiply as they
are seized.*

**SUN TZU**

You're the blacksmith of
your own happiness.

**SWEDISH PROVERB**

Every day holds the
possibility of a miracle.

**ELIZABETH DAVID**

**Keep smiling, because life is a beautiful thing and there's so much to smile about.**

MARILYN MONROE

One may walk over the
highest mountain one
step at a time.

**JOHN WANAMAKER**

Until you're ready to
look foolish, you'll never
have the possibility of
being great.

**CHER**

A life spent making mistakes is not only more honourable, but more useful than a life spent doing nothing.

**GEORGE BERNARD SHAW**

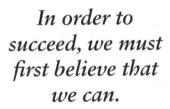

*In order to succeed, we must first believe that we can.*

NIKOS KAZANTZAKIS

# What we see depends mainly on what we look for.

JOHN LUBBOCK

Time goes on. So whatever
you're going to do, do it.
Do it now. Don't wait.

**ROBERT DE NIRO**

Find something you're
passionate about and
keep tremendously
interested in it.

**JULIA CHILD**

Life will always be
to a large extent
what we ourselves
make it.

**SAMUEL SMILES**

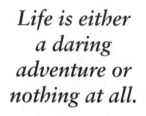

*Life is either
a daring
adventure or
nothing at all.*

HELEN KELLER

Plunge boldly into the
thick of life, and seize
it where you will, it is
always interesting.

**JOHANN WOLFGANG VON GOETHE**

The purpose of life is to live
it, to taste experience to the
utmost, to reach out eagerly
and without fear for newer
and richer experience.

**ELEANOR ROOSEVELT**

# Be yourself.
# The world worships
# the original.

INGRID BERGMAN

We do not remember
days, we remember
moments.

**CESARE PAVESE**

If you love life, don't
waste time, for time is
what life is made up of.

**BRUCE LEE**

There are no traffic jams
along the extra mile.

**ROGER STAUBACH**

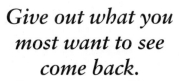

*Give out what you most want to see come back.*

ROBIN SHARMA

Put your heart, mind, and soul into even your smallest acts. This is the secret of success.

SIVĀNANDA SARASWATI

Change your
thoughts and you
change your world.

**NORMAN VINCENT PEALE**

Feelings are much like waves, we can't stop them from coming but we can choose which one to surf.

**JONATHAN MÅRTENSSON**

He is a wise man
who does not grieve
for the things which
he has not, but
rejoices for those
which he has.

**EPICTETUS**

*My best friend is
the one who brings
out the best in me.*

HENRY FORD

Every day is an
opportunity to make a
new happy ending.

**ANONYMOUS**

Life is really simple, but
we insist on making it
complicated.

**CONFUCIUS**

Do your little bit
of good where
you are; it's those
little bits of good
put together
that overwhelm
the world.

DESMOND TUTU

You can't use up
creativity. The more you
use, the more you have.

**MAYA ANGELOU**

The most important kind
of freedom is to be what
you really are.

JIM MORRISON

There was never a night
or a problem that could
defeat sunrise or hope.

**BERNARD WILLIAMS**

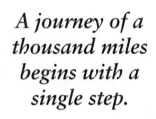

*A journey of a thousand miles begins with a single step.*

LAO TZU

A friend is one
who knows you
and loves you
just the same.

ELBERT HUBBARD

Understand that the
right to choose your own
path is a sacred privilege.
Use it. Dwell in possibility.

**OPRAH WINFREY**

Be eccentric now.
Don't wait for old
age to wear purple.

**REGINA BRETT**

Always be a first-rate
version of yourself,
instead of a second-
rate version of
somebody else.

**JUDY GARLAND**

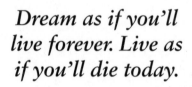

*Dream as if you'll live forever. Live as if you'll die today.*

**JAMES DEAN**

The best and most beautiful
things in the world cannot be
seen or even touched – they
must be felt with the heart.

**HELEN KELLER**

The secret of happiness
is the determination
to be happy always,
rather than wait for outer
circumstances to make
one happy.

**J. DONALD WALTERS**

Your present
circumstances
don't determine
where you can
go; they merely
determine where
you start.

NIDO QUBEIN

Only those who will
risk going too far
can possibly find out
how far one can go.

**T. S. ELIOT**

Cherish your visions and your dreams as they are the children of your soul; the blueprints of your ultimate achievements.

**NAPOLEON HILL**

When you have a
dream, you've got to
grab it and never let go.

**CAROL BURNETT**

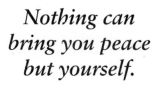

*Nothing can bring you peace but yourself.*

RALPH WALDO EMERSON

If we all did the things we are capable of, we would literally astound ourselves.

THOMAS EDISON

Let your hopes, not your
hurts, shape your future.

**ROBERT H. SCHULLER**

Hope is a talent
like any other.

**STORM JAMESON**

A friend is someone
who gives you total
freedom to be yourself.

**JIM MORRISON**

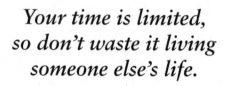

*Your time is limited,*
*so don't waste it living*
*someone else's life.*

**STEVE JOBS**

You ask me what I
came into this life
to do, I will tell you: I
came to live out loud.

**ÉMILE ZOLA**

When you dance to your
own rhythm, life taps its
toes to your beat.

**TERRI GUILLEMETS**

If you do not **change direction**, you may end up where you are heading.

**LAO TZU**

He who trims himself to
suit everyone will soon
whittle himself away.

**RAYMOND HULL**

Let your soul stand cool
and composed before
a million universes.

**WALT WHITMAN**

Life is not measured by
the number of breaths
you take, but by the
moments that take your
breath away.

**ANONYMOUS**

*Look at life through the windshield, not the rear-view mirror.*

**BYRD BAGGETT**

You are always free to change your mind and choose a different future, or a different past.

RICHARD BACH

First say to yourself
what you would be;
and then do what
you have to do.

**EPICTETUS**

We will always tend
to fulfil our own
expectation of
ourselves.

**BRIAN TRACY**

Life begins at the end of
your comfort zone.

**NEALE DONALD WALSCH**

*Success is due less to ability than to zeal.*

CHARLES BUXTON

To be yourself in a world
that is constantly trying
to make you something
else is the greatest
accomplishment.

**RALPH WALDO EMERSON**

The purpose of life is to
be happy.

**DALAI LAMA**

# We must accept finite disappointment, but never lose infinite hope.

MARTIN LUTHER KING JR

Life is short. Kiss
slowly, laugh
insanely, love truly
and forgive quickly.

**PAULO COELHO**

In a gentle way, you
can shake the world.

**MAHATMA GANDHI**

If you have good
thoughts they will shine
out of your face like
sunbeams and you will
always look lovely.

**ROALD DAHL**

*What great
thing would you
attempt if you
knew you could
not fail?*

ROBERT H. SCHULLER

To change
one's life:
1. Start immediately.
2. Do it flamboyantly.
3. No exceptions.

WILLIAM JAMES

Every moment is
a fresh beginning.

**T. S. ELIOT**

Very little is needed to
make a happy life; it
is all within yourself, in
your way of thinking.

**MARCUS AURELIUS**

Sometimes it's the
smallest decisions
that can change
your life forever.

**KERI RUSSELL**

*Most of us spend our lives as if we had another one in the bank.*

**BEN IRWIN**

The most important
thing is to enjoy your
life – to be happy – it's
all that matters.

**AUDREY HEPBURN**

Life is ten per cent
what happens to you
and ninety per cent
how you respond to it.

**LOU HOLTZ**

# The greatest sweetener of human life is Friendship.

JOSEPH ADDISON

Those who bring
sunshine into the lives
of others cannot keep
it from themselves.

**J. M. BARRIE**

Self-confidence is the
first requisite to great
undertakings.

**SAMUEL JOHNSON**

Good friends are like
stars... you don't always
see them but you know
they're always there.

**ANONYMOUS**

*Energy and persistence conquer all things.*

BENJAMIN FRANKLIN

**Believe** with all of your heart that you **will do** what you were made to do.

ORISON SWETT MARDEN

They always say time
changes things, but
you actually have to
change them yourself.

**ANDY WARHOL**

Don't be afraid to go out on a limb. That's where the fruit is.

**ANONYMOUS**

We have more
possibilities available
in each moment
than we realise.

**THÍCH NHẤT HẠNH**

*Change brings
opportunity.*

NIDO QUBEIN

Believe you can and
you're halfway there.

**THEODORE ROOSEVELT**

Smooth seas do not
make skilful sailors.

**AFRICAN PROVERB**

If you don't
like something,
change it; if you
can't change it,
change the way
you think about it.

MARY ENGELBREIT

Think big thoughts but
relish small pleasures.

**H. JACKSON BROWN JR**

If you change the way
you look at things,
the things you look at
change.

**WAYNE DYER**

Turn your face
toward the sun
and the shadows
will fall behind you.

**MAORI PROVERB**

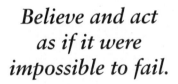

*Believe and act as if it were impossible to fail.*

CHARLES F. KETTERING

# Be happy for this moment. This moment is your life.

OMAR KHAYYÁM

Make each day
your masterpiece.

**JOHN WOODEN**

Become a possibilitarian. No matter how dark things seem to be or actually are, raise your sights and see possibilities.

**NORMAN VINCENT PEALE**

If opportunity doesn't
knock, build a door.

**MILTON BERLE**

*A loving heart is the truest wisdom.*

**CHARLES DICKENS**

The future depends on
what we do in the present.

MAHATMA GANDHI

If you're interested in
finding out more about our
books, find us on Facebook at
**Summersdale Publishers** and follow
us on Twitter at **@Summersdale**.

**www.summersdale.com**